BY CEZAR MARCILIO

# HAVEN'T
# WE MET
# BEFORE?

**ROBB**
ENTERTAINMENT
ROBBENT.COM

**ROBB**
PUBLISHING
BOOK.XROBB.COM

Haven't We Met Before? is a story about hope and how people approach and distance themselves from each other through their decisions and attitudes. In the future, corporations and politicians put inside of citizens' minds the idea that better days are coming; while they believe this, they don't have another alternative except to wait, wait, and wait a little more for illusory opportunities in endless lines. They have become used to an apathetic life while rich men become richer with their works and their waiting. In this depressive society, some characters show their feelings about the strangeness of the world around them. Jeff is an excitable guy, full of energy, hope, and ideas to improve his life. Together with his friends Brian and Thompson, he has tried many ways to leave Hope city. Daisy is a depressed and troubled prostitute, with many secrets and much anguish locked within. She lives her days without knowing what to do to alleviate her pain. Each decision these people make affects each of the others, showing us how strangers' acts can directly affect our lives. Pain, lies, and death are parts of this story about the quest for hope.

I'M HERE TO TALK ABOUT A CITY. A CITY I'VE BEEN WATCHING... TRYING TO UNDERSTAND. AT FIRST GLANCE, IT MAY LOOK LIKE ANY OTHER CITY, BUT IF WE LOOK CLOSER, IT'S AN ENTIRELY DIFFERENT WORLD...A WORLD ORGANIZED BY **LINES**. IN THIS NOT TOO DISTANT FUTURE, CIVIL WARS, UNEMPLOYMENT AND A GROWING POPULATION HAVE FORCED CITY LEADERS TO ADOPT A SYSTEM IN ORDER TO ORGANIZE THEIR POPULATION. THESE CITIES ARE KNOWN CALLED... **"HOPE CITIES"**.

**AFTER GRADUATING FROM HIGH SCHOOL**, THOSE WHO DO NOT MEET EXPECTATIONS TO EARN BETTER JOBS, HAVE PROFESSIONAL QUALIFICATIONS OR MAKE ENOUGH MONEY TO GO TO A UNIVERSITY WITHIN ONE YEAR ARE KEPT IN THESE CITIES. IN ORDER TO LEAVE, THEY MUST STAY HERE UNTIL THEY AFFORD ENOUGH **CREDITS**. ONCE THIS IS OBTAINED THEY MAY TRAVEL BACK TO THEIR ORIGINAL CITIES WHERE THE LINE SYSTEM DOES NOT EXIST. LET ME TRY TO CLARIFY THIS FURTHER.

IMAGINE LIVING HERE. THE GOVERNMENT ROUTES YOU TO THIS CITY AND THERE YOU RECEIVE A **HOPE CARD**. EVERYTHING YOU CONSUME, EARN AND SPEND IS THROUGH THIS CARD. YOU CANNOT LOSE IT. HERE, THERE IS **NO MONEY** - ONLY YOUR HOPE CARD.

**EVERY DAY** YOU MUST TAKE ON A DIFFERENT FORM OF EMPLOYMENT AND WAIT IN THE EMPLOYMENT LINES. THERE ARE LINES TO ALMOST EVERY TEDIOUS JOB IMAGINABLE: "SCREW TIGHTENER," DRESSMAKER, TYPIST, MECHANIC...

... SUGAR PACKERS AND KNIFE SHARPENERS. THERE ARE LINES FOR BAKING, GLUING SHOE SOLES, FIXING PIECES OF APPARATUS TOGETHER...

MOST JOBS DO NOT REQUIRE EXPERIENCE OR PRIOR KNOWLEDGE. HOWEVER, THE JOBS TEND TO BE **REPETITIVE**. ALL SERVICES THAT THE ORDINARY CITIES DO NOT WANT ARE DEPLOYED TO THE HOPE CITIES.

THE LINES ARE ABOUT AN HOUR AND A HALF WAIT BEFORE YOU CAN ACTUALLY START WORKING. YOU MUST WORK AT LEAST THREE HOURS DURING YOUR SHIFT IN ORDER TO **ACCUMULATE CREDITS** FOR YOUR HOPE CARD.

AFTER YOU LEAVE THE WORKPLACE, YOU'LL TYPICALLY DEVELOP AN APPETITE. THERE ARE **LINES** SET UP IN MULTIPLE PLACES TO RECEIVE A MEAL. LINES FOR COFFEE, SANDWICHES, ICE CREAM, AND EVEN BEER.

OF COURSE, ALL OF THE CITIZENS PAY WITH THEIR HOPE CARD. ONCE MORE, YOU NEED TO WAIT TO EAT. FROM HERE, YOU'VE SPENT SIX HOURS OF YOUR DAY. BUT IT DOESN'T END THERE. AFTER YOUR MEAL, YOU NEED TO SEEK ANOTHER LINE FOR ANOTHER JOB.

THE CITIZENS CAN'T WORK IN ANY GIVEN AREA MORE THAN TWICE A DAY, BUT THEY CAN WORK THE SAME JOB IN ANOTHER PLACE. SO, MY FRIEND, IT LOOKS LIKE YOU NEED TO SPEND ABOUT TWO MORE HOURS IN ANOTHER LINE AND THREE MORE HOURS WORKING ANOTHER JOB.

WHEN YOU ACCUMULATE THOUSANDS OF CREDITS ON YOUR HOPE CARD, YOU CAN APPLY FOR AUTHORIZATION TO LEAVE THE HOPE CITY AND GO TO A NORMAL CITY.

YOU MUST WORK A LOT TO SAVE UP ENOUGH CREDITS AND YOU HAVE TO SPEND AS LITTLE AS YOU CAN. SINCE IT'S VERY DIFFICULT TO DO THAT, MANY PEOPLE HAVE GOTTEN USED TO A LIFESTYLE INDUCED BY THE GOVERNMENT AND LARGE CORPORATIONS.

THEY LIVE REPEATING THEIR LIVES, ONLY WAITING FOR BETTER DAYS, AS IF IT WAS A FARAWAY DREAM. A DREAM AMIDST A SEA OF HOPE...NAY, A SEA OF LINES.

IF YOU WERE TO ASK IF THERE WERE ANYTHING FUN TO DO HERE. YOU'D BE SURPRISED TO FIND THAT THERE ACTUALLY IS. THERE ARE LINES TO PARTIES, TO MOVIE THEATRES, MALLS, AND, OF COURSE...

YOU HAD TO SEE HER FACE! I ALMOST GOT HER WHEN THE OTHERS IN LINE STARTED TO DISTURB US.

YEAH, IT WAS RIGHT AT THE MOMENT WHEN SHE WAS WAITING TO ESCAPE.

HAHAHAHAHAHA...

NO, THERE WAS DEFINITELY LOVE IN THE AIR! WE WILL SEE EACH OTHER AGAIN. I CAN FEEL IT.

AND THEN WHAT WOULD HAPPEN? CERTAINLY SHE WOULD END UP DUMPING YOU... SOME "ROMANCE".

THE TALLEST GUY IS **BRIAN**, A REALLY NICE GUY. HE SUPPORTS JEFF IN ALL HIS PLANS. THE GUY IN THE MIDDLE IS **THOMPSON**. NOBODY UNDERSTANDS HIM. HIS FATHER IS A RICH MAN WHO COULD EASILY GET HIM OUT OF HOPE CITY BUT DOESN'T. THOMPSON'S FATHER, **HARRY THOMPSON**, IS AN OWNER OF A FACTORY THAT MANUFACTURES AND DESIGNS GUN PARTS.

HE IS ONE OF THE BOSSES OF THE GUN MANUFACTURING COMPANY LOCATED WITHIN THE HOPE CITIES. HE LIVES HERE, BUT HE **DOESN'T NEED TO FACE LINES**. THE BOSS CAN LEAVE THE HOPE CITY ANYTIME HE WANTS. HE USUALLY VISITS OR LIVES IN HOPE CITY JUST FOR BUSINESS. HIS BUSINESSES, HOWEVER, **AREN'T VERY ETHICAL**.

BRIAN'S FATHER, **MR. HANK**, RUNS HIS OWN COMPANY TOO, MANUFACTURING WINDOWS. IT'S A LITTLE COMPANY WITH MANY BILLS AND TAXES TO PAY. IF HE WERE TO LOSE ANY OF HIS PROFIT, HE WOULD LOSE HIS POSITION AS A BOSS, AND THE GOVERNMENT WOULD ROUTE HIM TO THE LINES.

GIVE ME SOME TIME, GUYS. HER AND I WILL HAVE SEX.

HIS SALARY IS ENOUGH JUST TO KEEP HIS POSITION AND HIS COMPANY. BECAUSE OF THAT, HE **CAN'T HELP HIS SON**. HE'S A SOLITARY WIDOWER, WHO OFTEN WORRIES ABOUT HIS ONLY SON.

HEY, **DAISY**. HAVEN'T SEEN YOU WORKING MUCH LATELY. IF YOU KEEP THIS UP, YOU'LL NEVER LEAVE THIS DAMN CITY.

THIS IS **DAISY**, BUT SOME CALL HER NAMES LIKE HOOKER, BITCH, EASY, OR "PRINCESS OF PLEASURE."

ACCORDING TO WHAT CUSTOMERS HAVE SAID, HER BODY HAS CAUSED EVERY MAN TO RAISE HIS HANDS TO THE SKY AND THANK GOD FOR THEIR BALLS. SHE IS A VERY SEXY WOMAN. HOWEVER, IN THE LAST FEW DAYS, SHE HAS BEEN **UPSET**, WHICH IS COMMON HERE IN HOPE CITY. SHE IS ALWAYS WEARING HEAVY CLOTHING AND A BANDANA TO LOOK LESS BEAUTIFUL.

SORRY **PHOEBE**.

WHEN **DEPRESSION** KNOCKS ON YOUR DOOR, IT'S IMPOSSIBLE NOT TO LET HIM IN. I HATE THIS CITY...

THE PROBLEM IS THAT YOU LET THE **DEPRESSION** KNOCK ON YOUR DOOR, COME IN YOUR HOUSE, PLACE HIS HAND ON YOUR ASS AND SHIT IN YOUR BATHROOM WITH THE DOOR OPEN.

**FUCK**, DAISY! EVERYONE HATES THIS CITY...

THE PROSTITUTES CAN WORK THE SAME JOB **EVERY DAY** AT THE SAME PLACE. BEYOND THIS IS A LEGALIZED SERVICE. IT REQUIRES A LOT OF PHYSICAL ATTRIBUTES.

I KNOW.

...BUT BEING DEPRESSED DOESN'T IMPROVE YOUR SITUATION.

AND LOOK AT US. WE'RE **HOT**!

IF WE DO OUR WORK WELL AND GET SOME GOOD TIPS, WE CAN LEAVE THIS SHITTY PLACE.

... I'M NOT SURE. I NEED TO THINK ABOUT IT.

EXCELLENT! YOU CAN SHOW UP ON ANY THURSDAY. HE HAS SO MANY CREDITS.

IT'S IN 6B FLAT. IT'LL BE GOOD FOR YOU TO EARN SOME CREDITS AGAIN. THINK ABOUT IT.

I'LL CATCH YOU LATER!

NOW I NEED TO WORK. THERE ARE "KIDS" HUNGRY FOR ME.

BYE!

DEPRESSING, DISPIRITED, TEDIOUS. THESE ALL DESCRIBE THE FEELINGS FOUND WITHIN **HOPE CITY**.

IF THERE WAS A LINE FOR OBTAINING HAPPINESS, CERTAINLY IT WOULD BE THE LONGEST.

AFTER EVERY WEEK PASSES, THE CITIZENS MUST CHANGE THEIR **ACCOMMODATIONS**. IT'S ONE MORE WAY FOR THE GOVERNMENT TO KEEP THE PEOPLE IN LINE AND THE ECONOMY IN MOTION. OF COURSE, YOU ARE ALLOWED TO CHOOSE THE KIND OF ACCOMMODATION.

IF YOU WANT TO SAVE CREDITS, THERE ARE CHEAP ACCOMMODATIONS AVAILABLE, AS LONG AS YOU'RE NOT WORRIED ABOUT SLEEPING WITH **SEVERAL PEOPLE** IN THE SAME BEDROOM.

MORE PEOPLE ARE WORKING, MORE PEOPLE ARE SPENDING CREDITS, MORE CONFORMED PEOPLE. ALL THE CREDITS FROM HOPE CITIES BECOME MONEY OUTSIDE, IN THE NORMAL CITIES. IN OTHER WORDS, THE HOPE CITY'S ECONOMY MAKES **HUGE MONEY** TO BUSINESSES **OUT THERE**, BUSINESSES OF PEOPLE WHO DON'T CARE ABOUT THE PEOPLE IN HOPE CITY.

MR. THOMPSON'S FACTORY

ANOTHER PROFESSION THAT DOESN'T NEED TO FACE LINES ARE THE **LAWMAKERS**. IT'S NOT COMMON FOR CRIME TO OCCUR IN THIS CITY. BUT WHEN IT HAPPENS, THEY'RE USUALLY **HARD** TO INVESTIGATE.

DETECTIVE **MILLER** AND HIS SIDEKICK **CANDY** ARE TWO "CORRUPTION PROOF" LAWMAKERS.

THEY TREAT ALL INVESTIGATIONS WITH ZERO TOLERANCE, ESPECIALLY THE INVESTIGATIONS ABOUT MR. THOMPSON'S BUSINESS.

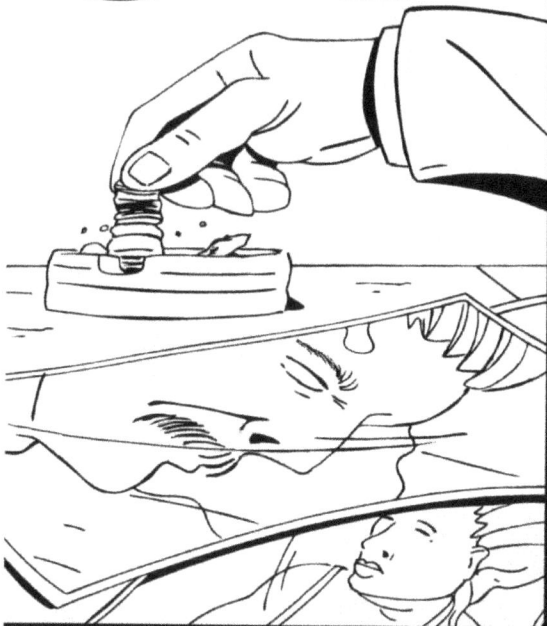

I CAME HERE BECAUSE YOU PROMISED ME A SUCCESSFUL **BUSINESS**.

YOU'RE BLUNT. I LIKE THAT. BUT I'M NOT ASKING FOR YOUR HELP. I WANT TO HIRE YOU FOR YOUR SERVICES, BRIAN.

YOUR SON IS A FRIEND WHO I APPRECIATE, I'M **NOT SURE** I CAN SAY THE SAME ABOUT YOU.

WE CAN TALK WHILE WE WALK THROUGH **THE SEWERS** HERE. COME ON.

IT'S BEEN A LONG TIME SINCE I'VE WALKED WITHOUT A MILLION PEOPLE IN FRONT OF ME.

THERE ARE A LOT OF GALLERIES AND CORRIDORS HIDDEN UNDER THIS FACTORY.

A COUPLE OF MINUTES AGO SOME DETECTIVES WERE IN MY OFFICE, **BLAMING ME** FOR GUN TRAFFICKING AND MURDERS OUTSIDE OF THIS CITY.

HUMANKIND IS FUNNY. THEY HAVE ONLY TWO PATHS TO FOLLOW IN LIFE. A GOOD ONE AND A BAD ONE. WHEN THEY CHOOSE THE BAD ONE, BAD THINGS START TO HAPPEN.

THEY BLAME DRUGS, MONEY, GUNS, GOD, BUT NEVER **THEMSELVES**. IT'S SO DAMN SELFISH, IN MY OPINION.

WHAT'RE YOU GETTING AT?

I WANT YOU TO **KILL** SOMEONE FOR ME.

ARE YOU CRAZY, MAN?

WHAT MAKES YOU THINK I WOULD DO THAT? I WOULD NEVER...

FOR A MAN WHO USED TO DO **PETTY CRIMES**, YOU LOOK PRETTY SCARED NOW. YOU DON'T KNOW HOW HARD IT IS TO TRUST SOMEONE TO DO JOBS LIKE THIS.

THAT WAS WHEN I NEEDED TO HELP MY **FATHER**, BUT NOW I PREFER...

YOU PREFER NOTHING, MY FRIEND. YOU'RE ONE MORE POOR GUY WALKING IN A LINE, BEGGING FOR CREDITS IN EACH **FUCKING JOB**.

YOUR FATHER IS A WIDOWER AND AN ALMOST **BANKRUPT MAN**. DON'T LIE TO YOURSELF. HE STILL NEEDS YOUR HELP. LET ME EXPLAIN MY SITUATION AND THE PROPOSAL.

HIDDEN IN THESE GALLERIES, SOME OF MY DAMN EMPLOYEES **ARE DEALING GUN PARTS**, UNDER MY NOSE. I WOULD LIKE TO DEAL ENTIRE GUNS, NOT JUST PARTS OF THEM. BUT SELLING PARTS IS THE ONLY WAY TO MAKE CREDITS AND MONEY OUTSIDE OF HERE.

MY CUSTOMERS ARE FAR AWAY FROM HERE, FAR AWAY FROM THE COPS EVEN. THE PROBLEM IS THESE MEN ARE DEALING GUNS TO THE NEIGHBORING TOWNS. THAT'S **A BIG MISTAKE**.

THE GUNMAKING BUSINESS WAS **BANNED** A LONG TIME AGO.

NOW JUST MYSELF, COPS AND THE MILITARY HAVE AUTHORIZATION TO DEAL GUNS IN THIS CITY. IN EVERY CRIME SCENE INVESTIGATION THAT HAPPENS IN THE NEIGHBORING TOWNS, THE COPS ARE FINDING GUNS MADE **FROM MY FACTORY**.

WHO DO YOU THINK THE LAW **BLAMES** FOR EACH MURDER THAT HAPPENS IN THESE NEIGHBORING TOWNS?

THEY KEEP THEMSELVES **HOODED** AS THEY'RE DEALING GUNS TO AVOID BEING SEEN BY THE POLICE. ONE OF THEM HAS A WAY OF GOING OUT TO THE NEIGHBORING CITIES AND COMING BACK HERE. HE IS MAKING *GOOD MONEY* AND IS SAVING A **LOT OF CREDITS** DOING IT.

HE OR SHE COULD BE A COP, A BUSINESS PERSON, OR A MEMBER OF THE MILITARY. I DON'T KNOW. BUT THIS PERSON IS **DUSTING MY IMAGE** IN FRONT OF THE LAW.

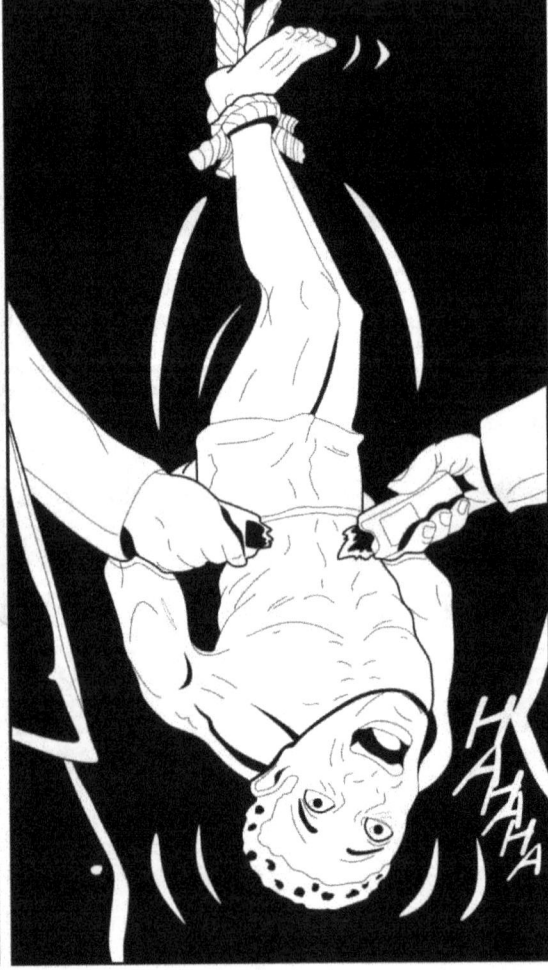

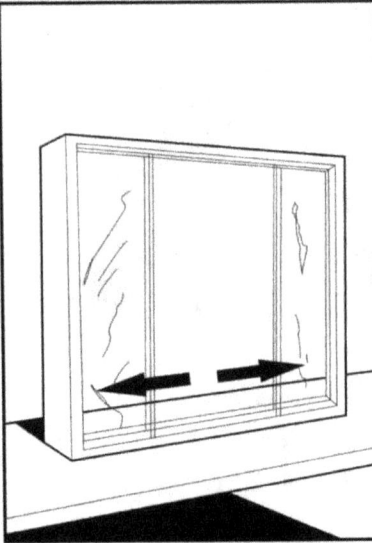

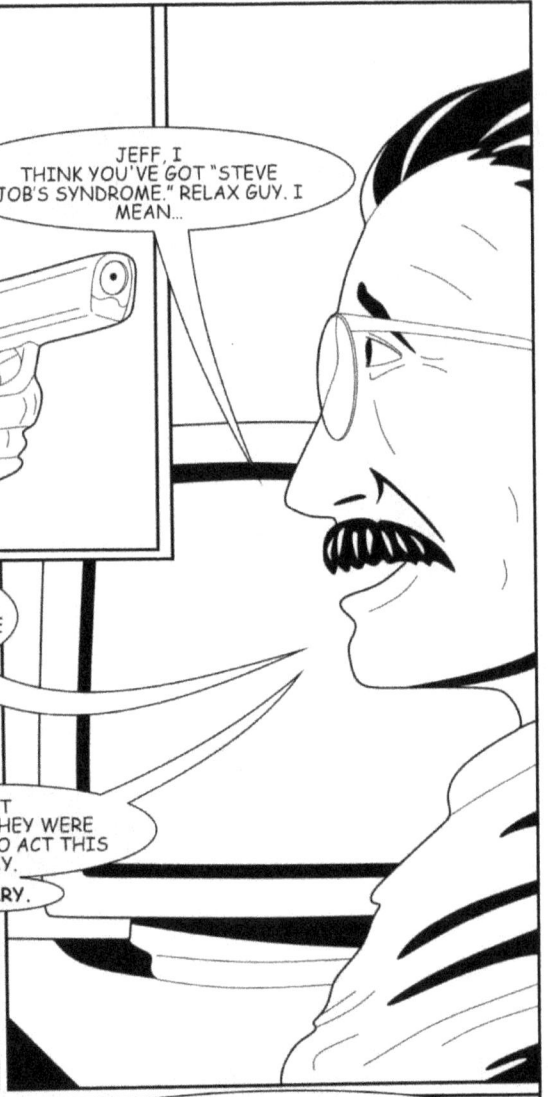

I CAN'T TURN INTO ONE OF THEM. I PREFER TO BE ALIEN RATHER THAN AN UNMOTIVATED **ZOMBIE** SPENDING MY DAYS BEING MISERABLE.

IF I LET MYSELF DOWN, WHAT WOULD HAPPEN NEXT? **SUICIDE?** NO. I'M BETTER THAN THAT...

I JUST WANT TO LOVE SOMEONE...

I JUST WANT TO STAY WITH MY FRIENDS LONGER.

I JUST WANT TO WORK WITH MY IDEAS. IS THAT ASKING TOO MUCH?

MY WRISTS ARE ACHING FROM ALL THE DOORS I'VE KNOCKED ON TRYING TO SHOW MY INVENTIONS.

MY TONGUE'S GONE DRY FROM EXPLAINING ABOUT ALL OF MY INVENTIONS. I'M TIRED OF HEARING THINGS LIKE, "NEXT TIME," "MAYBE" OR "SORRY, WE CAN'T HELP YOU."

I END UP THINKING ABOUT WHY I DIDN'T REACH MY GOALS. WHAT DID I MISS IN MYSELF? MR. HANK WAS RIGHT. WE WERE EDUCATED TO STOP CARING ABOUT PEOPLE. ALMOST EVERYBODY WANTS TO EARN A LITTLE SALARY AND CONTINUE ON WITH THEIR SIMPLE LIVES.

IT'S NOT ABOUT LOVE. IT'S ABOUT OUR RELATIONSHIP.
YOU'RE TWENTY YEARS YOUNGER THAN ME, YOU'RE A **PROSTITUTE**. WHAT DO YOU THINK MY SON AND MY FAMILY OUT THERE WILL THINK ABOUT US?
HOW DO I KNOW YOU WILL NOT LEAVE ME FOR A YOUNGER MAN ONCE WE LEAVE HERE?
**I'M NOT A PROSTITUTE ANYMORE!**
I'M NOT A **PROSTITUTE** ANYMORE! ARE YOU THAT WORRIED ABOUT WHAT OTHERS WILL THINK OF YOU? **YOUR LOVE** FOR ME ISN'T ENOUGH TO BARE THAT?
I HAVE TO STAY HERE TO HELP MY SON. HE GOT INVOLVED IN SOME TROUBLE IN THE PAST. I DON'T WANT ANYMORE OF IT...
DO YOU LOVE ME?
DO YOU THINK I'M HERE TO TAKE ADVANTAGE OF YOU?

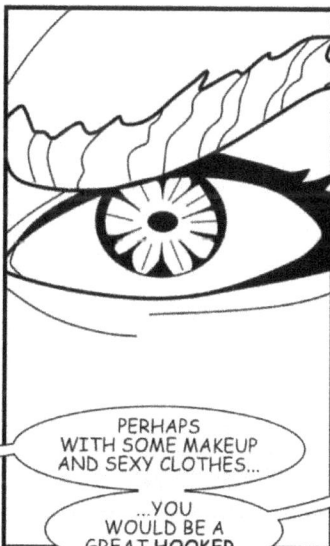

AND SURE, I WENT IN TO RESCUE HIM. WE GOT INTO SOME **TROUBLE** WHEN THE COPS GOT THERE THOUGH.

WE SPENT ABOUT THREE HOURS IN LINE JUST TO STAY IN JAIL FOR ANOTHER THREE HOURS. I SHOULD HAVE REMEMBERED THAT JUMPING A LINE IS CONSIDERED A **CRIME** HERE.

**LINE TO JAIL** →

YEAH, IT'S PROBABLY THE WORST **PUNISHMENT**.

HE STAYED MAD AT ME FOR A LONG TIME, BUT I JUST WANTED TO HELP HIM. I KNEW IT WAS MY FAULT AND IT WAS A **STUPID MISTAKE**.

BUT AFTER THAT, WE WOULD BRING UP OUR FIGHT AND LAUGH A LOT ABOUT **EACH PUNCH** WE COULD RECALL. IT FINISHED AS GOOD FUN.

WELL, I GUESS IN A CITY WHERE THERE'S NOTHING TO DO BUT WAIT IN LINE, TROUBLE LIKE THAT BECOMES THE **HIGHLIGHT** OF THE DAY.

I HAVEN'T HAD A FUN MOMENT LIKE THAT IN A LONG TIME.

I REMEMBER IT LIKE IT WAS YESTERDAY. I STILL CAN FEEL THE PUNCHES SOMETIMES.

**YEAH,** SOMETIMES WE NEED TROUBLE TO ADVANCE OUR LIVES.

EACH DAY THAT PASSES BY IS SO BORING THAT WE HAVE FORGOTTEN WHAT WE'RE ABLE TO DO. WE HAVE THE OPPORTUNITY TO CHANGE OUR LIVES, **BREAK LIMITS** AND GO WITHOUT FEAR.

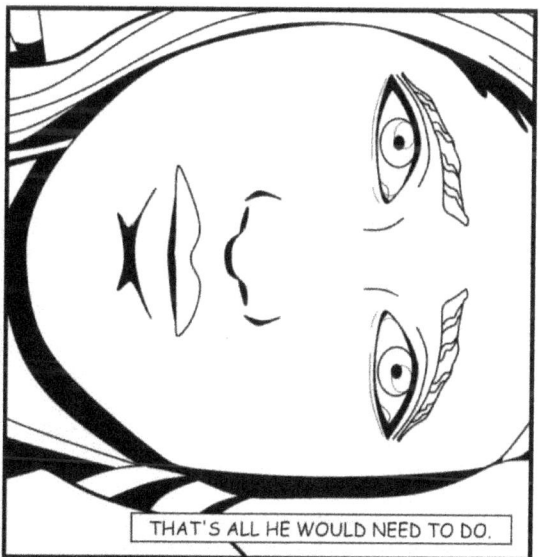

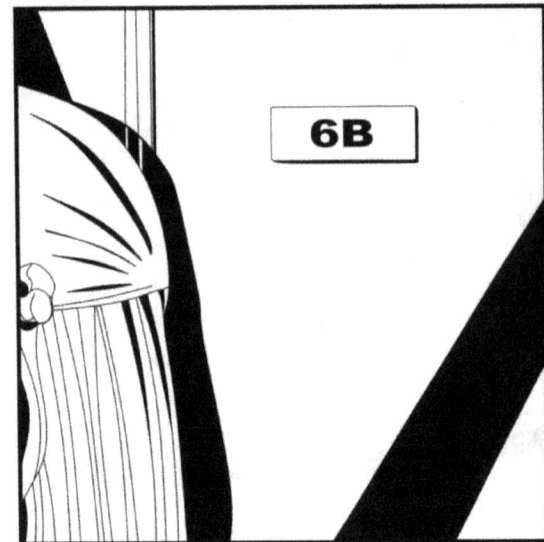

JUST TWO SHOTS. ONE IN THE TRAFFICKER'S HEAD AND ANOTHER ONE IN THE WHORE'S HEAD TO ENSURE THERE WON'T BE ANY WITNESSES. I HAVE A GOOD SHOT, EVEN IN THE DARK. I'VE DONE IT IN THE PAST.

BUILDING 358

6B FLAT

IT'S PAST.

IT DEPRESSES ME EVERY TIME I THINK ABOUT IT. THAT'S WHY I LIKE STAYING CLOSE TO MY FRIENDS.

THEY MAKE ME SMILE ALL THE TIME.

TRY TO DO SOMETHING BEYOND OUR LIMITS, I SAID. WHAT WAS I THINKING WHEN I SAID THAT?

OR WHAT WAS I THINKING WHEN I ACCEPTED THIS JOB?

THE ANSWER IS SIMPLE.

00:28 a.m

I NEED TO GET ENOUGH CREDITS TO HELP MY FATHER AND MAYBE TO HELP JEFF...

...AND WHERE HAS **JEFF** BEEN THIS AFTERNOON? I TRIED TO CALL HIM BUT HE DIDN'T ANSWER. I WANTED TO TALK WITH SOMEONE IN ORDER TO REMAIN CALM BEFORE THIS **MISSION** TONIGHT...

HE IS BUSY WITH ANOTHER ONE OF HIS INVENTIONS, I GUESS.

**FATHER?** WHERE IS MY FATHER?

... HE USUALLY DOESN'T COME BACK TO THE HOUSE **TOO LATE**.

IT DOESN'T MATTER RIGHT NOW, THE TIME HAS COME AND **I MUST GO**.

THANK THE LORD THIS PART OF THE CITY DOESN'T HAVE LINES AT NIGHT.

I **SWEAR**. THIS IS THE LAST TIME I'M DOING THIS.

THIS ONE IS FOR MY **FRIENDS**...

AND FOR MY **FATHER**.

I THINK I'M IN LOVE.

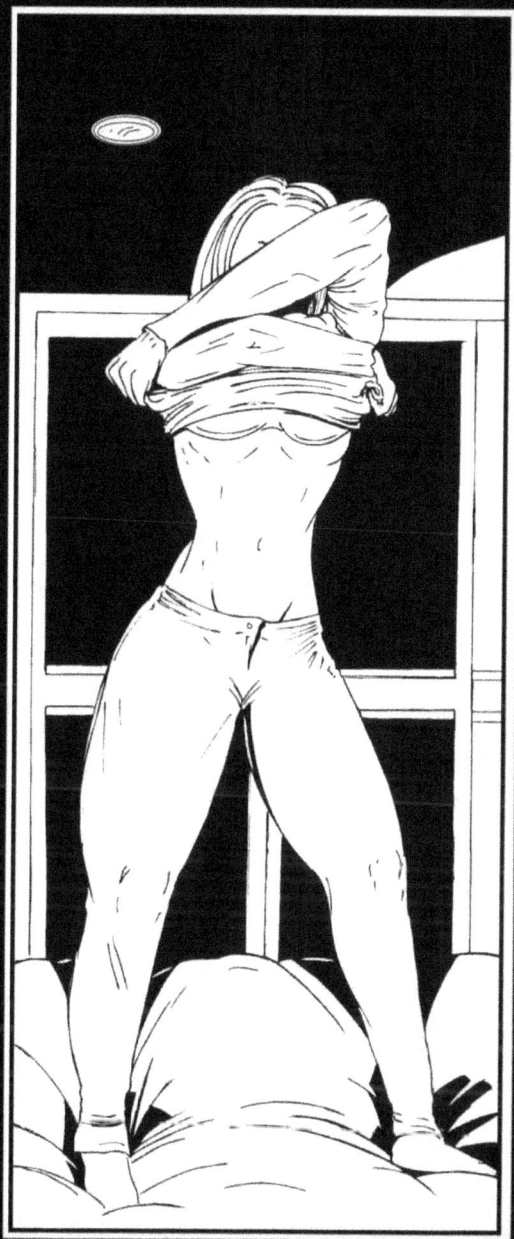

I DON'T HAVE WORDS TO DESCRIBE.

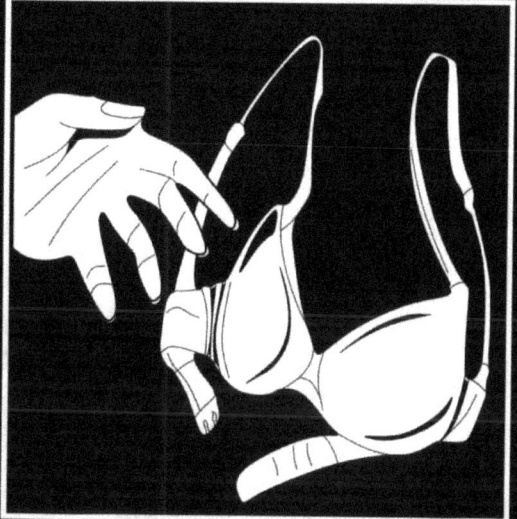

SHE LOVES ME.

SHE LOVES ME, I'M SURE OF IT.

WHOA...I'M FLYING...WOOOO!
IT DOESN'T EVEN FILL THE GAP BETWEEN MY TEETH!
MORE...MORE...
THIS IS SO PATHETIC. SUCKING A PENCIL WOULD GIVE ME MORE PLEASURE.
I'LL SUCK IT SO INTENSELY, THAT HE WON'T BE ABLE TO PISS FOR A WEEK.
THIS IS SO HUMILIATING, I DESERVE AN OSCAR FOR BEST ACTRESS.
YOU LOVE ME. I KNOW YOU LOVE ME.
THIS COCK DOESN'T REACH THE ROOF OF MY MOUTH BUT I HAVE TO PRETEND TO ENJOY IT... AND...
FUCK...I SWALLOWED.

JUST A DAMN TRAFFICKER AND A BITCH. I'M JUST CLEANING THE STREETS OF THESE PEOPLE.

JUST TWO SHOTS. I WON'T LOOK AT THEIR FACES. AND THEN I SWEAR NEVER TO DO IT AGAIN.

NO MORE. JUST **TWO SHOTS**.

THEN I'LL **STOP**.

THERE IT IS. AND IT'S ALMOST **2:00 AM**. THEY'RE PROBABLY TAKING A BREAK FROM HAVING SEX.

IF HE HAS MADE AS MUCH AS MR. THOMPSON SAYS FROM TRAFFICKING GUNS, HE WON'T BE IN A HURRY TO LEAVE.

HE'LL WANT TO **RELAX** AND ENJOY HIMSELF.

BUT IF HE HAS A **GUN**... **DAMNIT**, BRIAN, YOU'RE SO STUPID. WHY DIDN'T YOU THINK ABOUT THAT?

HE'S A **GUN TRAFFICKER**. OF COURSE HE HAS A GUN.

I CAN PLAN BETTER **NEXT WEEK**. WHEN THEY MEET AGAIN.

NO, I MUST DO THIS **NOW**.

I MUST BE CERTAIN THAT THEY ARE TOGETHER. THAT WAY IT WILL BE EASIER TO FINISH THE JOB.
6B
HEY BABY, IF YOU CAN DO THAT JUST WITH YOUR MOUTH, I CAN'T IMAGINE WHAT YOU CAN DO WITH THE REST OF YOUR BODY.
THAT WAS AMAZING.
LET'S WAIT A LITTLE BIT BEFORE WE GO AGAIN. I NEED TO RELAX MY COCK BEFORE I CAN GO AGAIN.
NO WORRIES, DEAR. WE HAVE A LONG AND UNFORGETTABLE NIGHT AHEAD OF US.
HE HAS THE COURAGE TO NAME IT A COCK. IT'S NOT GOING UP AGAIN FOR A WHILE...
ABSOLUTELY, MY PRINCESS. ALL OF THIS IS FOR YOU.
ALL OF THIS IS FOR YOU? GOSH, THIS DEFLATED COCK LEFT A BAD TASTE IN MY MOUTH.
I NEED TO BRUSH MY TEETH WITH SOAP OR SOMETHING NOW.
I HOPE THIS APARTMENT HAS JUST ONE ROOM LIKE MOST OF THE BUILDINGS HERE.

SOMETIMES WE NEED A LITTLE OPPORTUNITY TO CHANGE OUR LIVES. SOMETIMES WE NEED A LITTLE LIGHT TO GUIDE OUR PATH. BUT THIS LITTLE HELP SEEMS SO HARD TO GET.

NOBODY WANTS TO BEG FOR A BETTER LIFE. SOMETIMES WE JUST NEED A LITTLE PUSH TO PUT US ON THE RIGHT PATH.

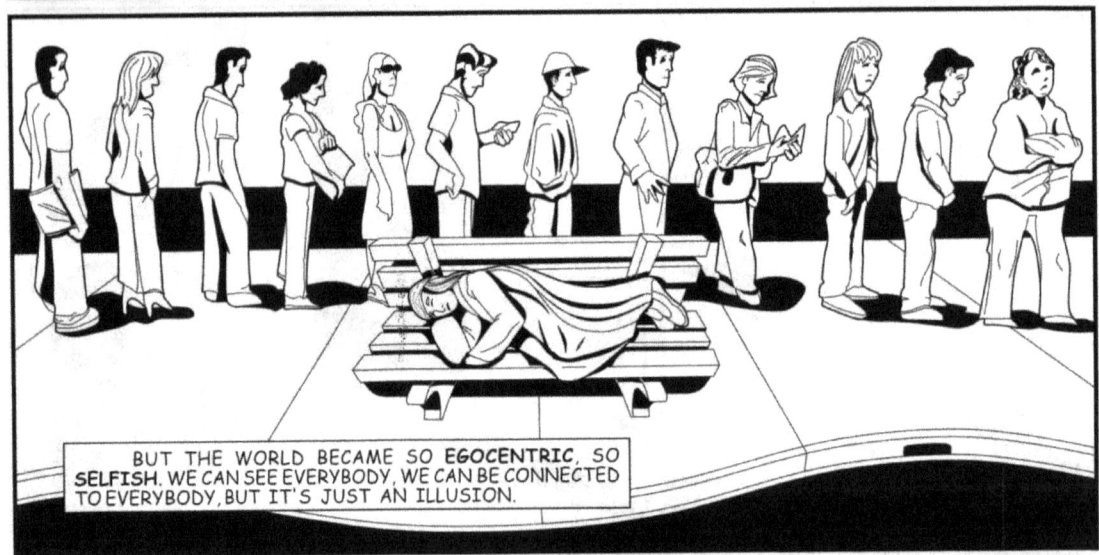

BUT THE WORLD BECAME SO EGOCENTRIC, SO SELFISH. WE CAN SEE EVERYBODY, WE CAN BE CONNECTED TO EVERYBODY, BUT IT'S JUST AN ILLUSION.

WE DON'T CARE ABOUT OTHERS. WE ONLY SEE OTHERS AS DISTRACTIONS.

WE DON'T WANT TO TOUCH THEIR HANDS, SEE WHAT THEY SEE OR FEEL THEIR FEELINGS.

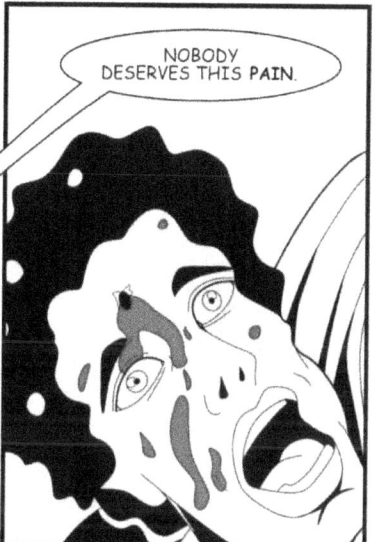

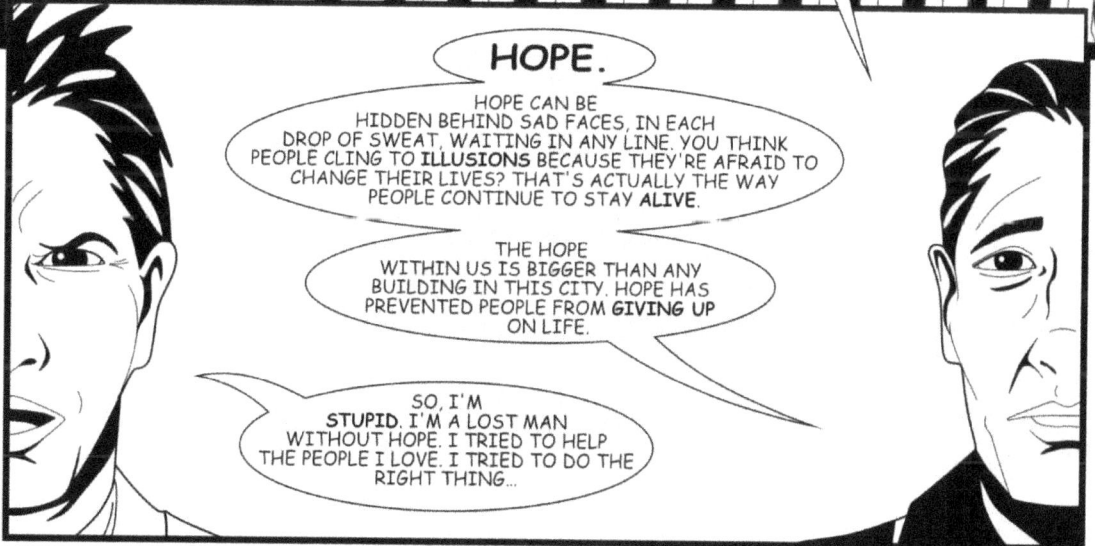

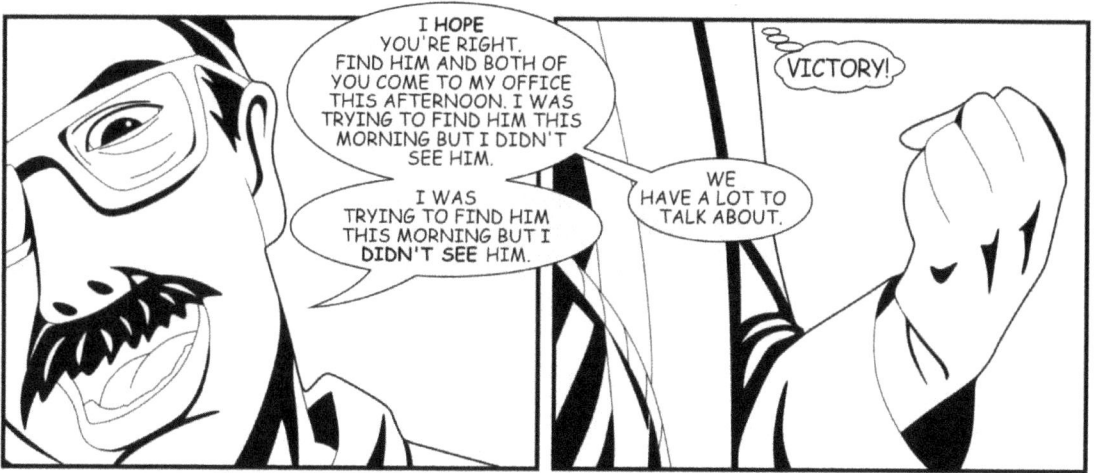

OHOOHO OHOOOHOO
LINE TO SEE SUICIDES
A SUICIDE!
IT'S BEEN "A HUNDRED" YEARS SINCE SOMEONE HAS COMMITTED SUICIDE. AND THIS DAY WAS STARTING OUT GREAT...
HEY, LET ME SEE THIS COWARD.
FUCK!
NO, THIS IS IMPOSSIBLE!
MY FRIEND.

MY BEST FRIEND...

WHY?

MOVE QUICKLY.

LET ME SEE.

WHY YOU?

HUMANITY IS **ODD**, WATCHING FROM HERE. THEY CREATE THEIR OWN TROUBLE, THEY WAIT FOR MORE TROUBLE AND THEY BLAME OTHERS

THEY **BLAME** THEIR GOVERNMENT, THEIR SYSTEM, THEIR BOSSES AND THEIR PARENTS. THEY BLAME GOD.

BUT THEY NEVER BLAME **THEMSELVES**. I SAY THAT FROM MY OWN EXPERIENCE.

THIS WEEK HAS BEEN DIFFERENT. AFTER **BRIAN** CAME HERE, TWO OTHER MEN ALSO CAME HERE TO JUMP.

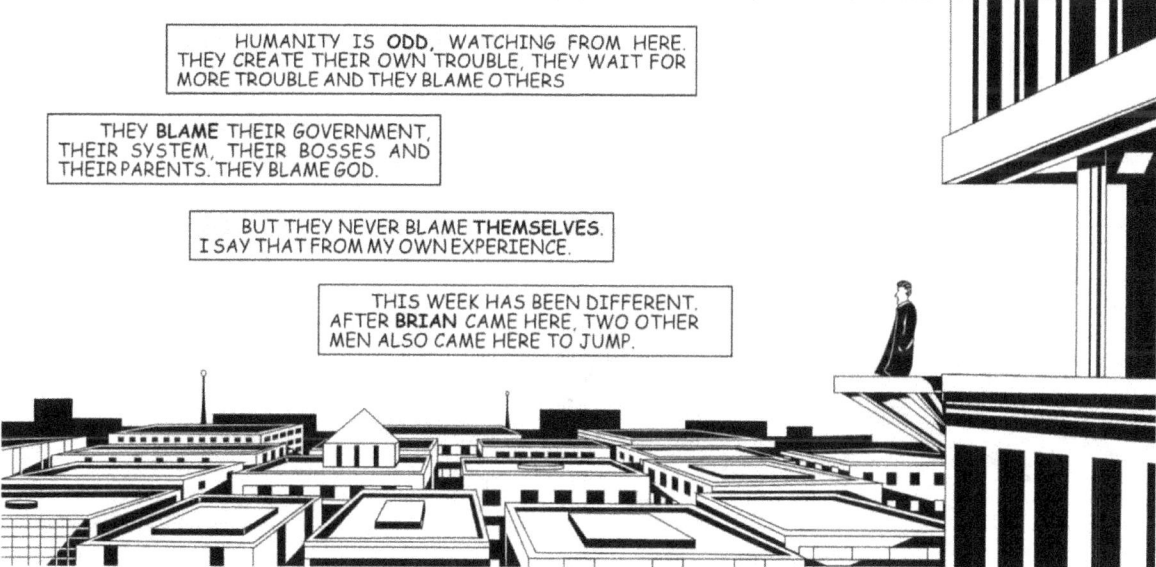

ONE OF THEM WAS A MAN WITH A MUSTACHE AND GLASSES. HE SAID HIS TWO MAIN REASONS TO LIVE WERE GONE.

AFTER THAT, HE WAS **GONE**.

MR. HANK

"Office closed indefinitely due to the passing of Mr. Hank."

I DIDN'T UNDERSTAND HIM IN THE MOMENT. BUT I FELT HIS PAIN WAS SO STRONG. THAT WAS STRANGE TO ME.

THE OTHER ONE WAS AN OLD, FAT, BEARDED MAN. HE WAS **REALLY SAD**. WE SPENT A LONG TIME TALKING. HE TOLD ME A STORY THAT HE KNEW. NAMES, DRAMAS, UNEXPECTED SITUATIONS, DEATHS.

HE WAS SO SORRY ABOUT WHAT HE DID THAT FOR A FEW SECONDS, I THOUGHT HE WOULDN'T JUMP. BUT HE SAID IT WAS TOO LATE AND HE JUMPED. LIKE HE WANTED TO KEEP HIS **WHOLE STORY** WITH ME.

THE NEXT DAY, **TWO LAWMAKERS** CAME HERE ASKING QUESTIONS.

NO MORE.

MY OTHER **FRIEND**.

I HOPE I DON'T SEE ANYMORE PEOPLE JUMPING FROM HERE.

I CAN'T BEAR IT.

YES, THIS MAY LOOK LIKE **ANY CITY**, BUT IT'S NOT

HERE I HAVE REALIZED THAT PEOPLE ARE WEAK AND FRIGHTENED. THEY'RE CONFORMED FROM THE SYSTEM, AS ROTTEN AS IT IS.

SOMETIMES SOMEONE LEAVES THE LINE AND REALIZES HOW SAD IT IS. THIS PERSON CAN COMPLAIN, **MAKES NOISE** AND TRIES TO DRAW THE ATTENTION OF OTHERS.

BUT IT LASTS FOR A SHORT TIME. THIS ONE IS **UNABLE TO KNOW** WHERE THE END AND THE BEGINNING OF THE LINE IS.

AFTER, THIS PERSON BECOMES BORED, THIS PERSON WILL THEN REALIZE THE HYPOCRISY OF THE WORLD, BUT WILL BE UNABLE TO FIND A WAY TO LEAVE IT.

SOMETIMES SOMEONE TRIES TO DO SOMETHING **BEYOND** HIS LIMIT.

BUT IN HIS FIRST FAILURE, GOES BACK TO THE LINE AND KEEPS TO HIMSELF, FEELING **SADDER** THAN BEFORE.

THEY HAVE LIVED IN AN **ILLUSION** INDUCED BY SOCIETY AND THEY WALK INSTINCTIVELY IN A LINE, AFRAID TO FACE REALITY.

AFRAID TO FIGHT FOR A BETTER LIFE. BECAUSE IT'S EASIER... EASIER TO WALK IN THE SAME DIRECTION THAT **EVERYBODY** ELSE IS GOING.

SNACK BAR

Cezar Marcilio is a Brazilian citizen currently residing in Los Angeles, CA, where he works as a freelance illustrator and writer. He's a graduate of history and has taken quite a few professional art courses. Also, he is always creating new projects and seeking ways to show his ideas to the world. His major influences are the books of Will Eisner and Alan Moore, and because of this, his stories explore the conscience of people in their quest for their goals and passions. "Haven't We Met Before?" is his debut book (graphic novel) where he takes the role as both the artist and the writer. The book shows us a story about hope and it is also a reflection of the first steps of its artist.

www.ingramcontent.com/pod-product-compliance
Lightning Source LLC
Chambersburg PA
CBHW081258040426
42452CB00014B/2556